APJ Abdul Kalam —The Missile Man of India

Dr. APJ Abdul Kalam is one of the most distinguished scientist of India. He is a renowned professor, aeronautical engineer and the chancellor of the Indian Institute of Space Science and Technology (IIST).

Dr. APJ Abdul Kalam served as the 11th President of India from 2002 to 2007. He is often referred as 'People's President'. He is also popularly known as the 'Missile Man of India', because of his extraordinary contribution in the development of Ballistic Missile project and Space Rocket Technology. He also worked as a scientist in ISRO and DRDO. He was awarded with the Bharat Ratna—India's highest civilian honour in 1997.

Birth and Early Years of Dr. Kalam's Life

Dr. APJ Abdul Kalam was born in Rameshwaram (in Tamilnadu) in a middle-class Muslim family on 15th October 1931. His father was Jainulabdeen and mother was Ashiamma. Dr. Kalam's full name is Avul Pakir Jainulabdeen. His father was a devout Muslim, who had good relations with the Rameshwaram temple priests. He used to rent his owned boats out to the local fishermen. He was a good friend of the Hindu religious leaders and school teachers of Rameshwaram.

During his childhood, Dr. Kalam lived very close to the sea. He developed a great passion for nature and sea. He used to spend a lot of time watching the waves of sea. His mother influenced him to a great extent in developing his talents in music and writing poetry.

Dr. Kalam's parents led a very simple lifestyle. They imbibed good moral values in their children. Dr. Kalam became religious at a very young age. He reads 'Quran' and 'Bhagwat Geeta' daily and strictly follows vegetarian diet. Dr. Kalam devoted his entire life in doing research work.

Dr. Kalam spent most of his childhood in financial problems. His education began in a rural primary school at Rameshwaram. Later, he was shifted to Ramnathpuram Missionary School.

Dr. Kalam started working at a very early age. To bear the expenses of his education, he worked as a newspaper hawker.

His teachers, parents and others noticed his efforts and brilliance. Some of his teachers even came forward to help him.

After completing his school education in 1954, he took his graduation degree in Physics from St. Joseph College, Tiruchirapalli. In 1957, Kalam completed Bachelor of Engg. in Aerospace engineering from Madras Institute of Technology. Later he obtained advanced master and doctorate degrees in his respected field from the same institute.

Dr. Kalam's Professional Life

After completing his third year at MIT, he joined Hindustan Aeronautics Limited (HAL), Bangalore as a trainee and worked on the piston and turbine engines. In 1958, he came out of Hindustan Aeronautics Limited as a graduate.

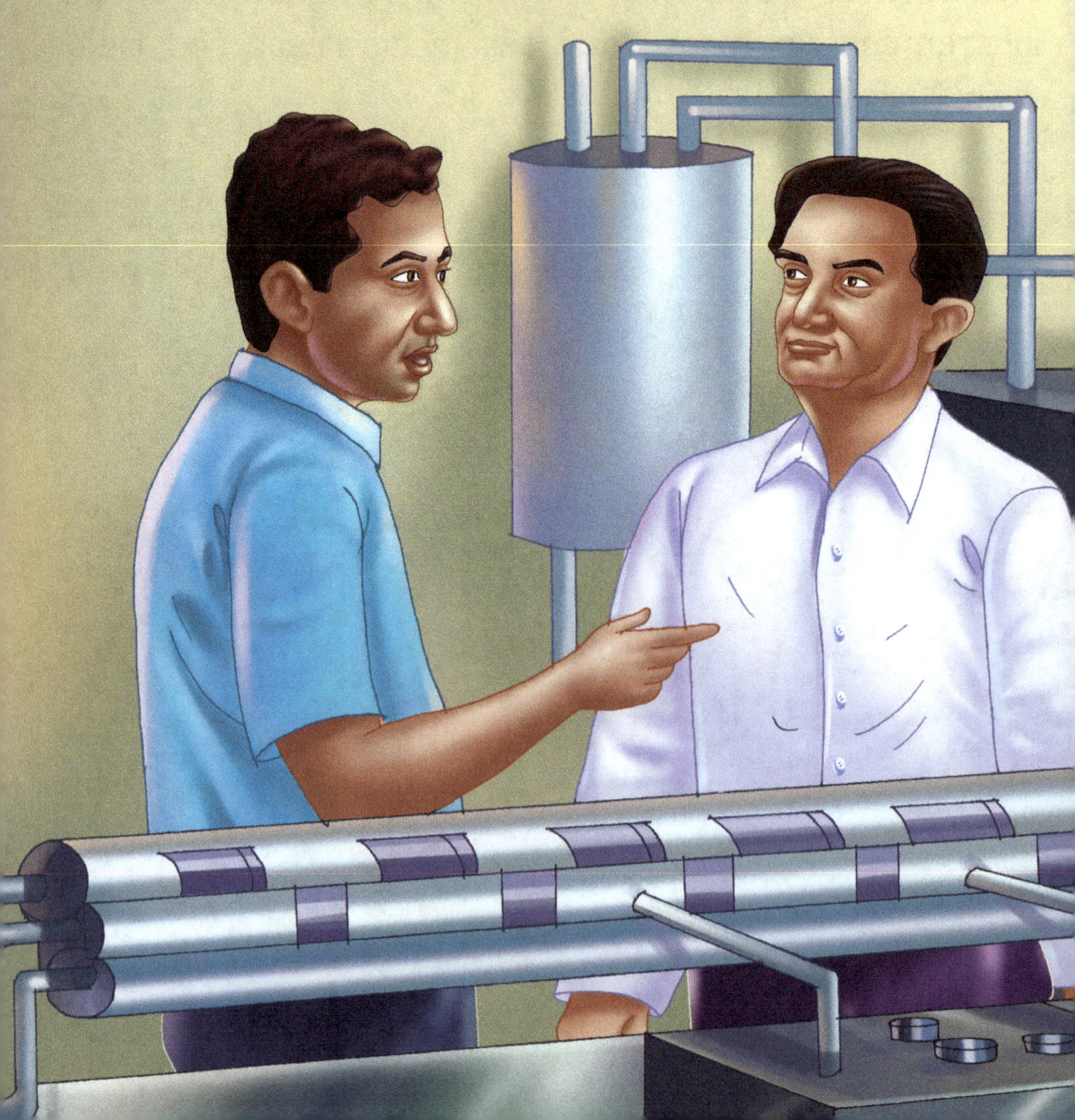

Thereafter, he got the opportunity to sewed at Indian Space Research Organisation (ISRO). After working on the several projects, he soon became a Project Director for India's first indigenous satellite launch vehicle (SLV-III) at Thumba.

The SLV-3 project was successful in placing Rohini—a scientific satellite—into orbit in July 1980 and was honoured with a Padma Bhushan in 1981. During this time, Dr. Kalam got to work with three great minds—Dr. Vikram Sarabhai, Professor Satish Dhawan and Dr. Brahm Prakash. He has also acknowledged these three people in his autobiography.

The second phase of Dr. Kalam's professional life started when he joined Defence Research Development Organisation (DRDO) in 1982. As Director of DRDO, he was entrusted with Integrated Guided Missile Development Program (IGMDP).

He played a major role in the development of many important Missiles like Nag, Akash, Trishul, Agni and Prithvi.

Three new laboratories for missile technologies were also developed during his tenure. His contributions in India's defence system are admirable.

Thereafter, Dr. Kalam worked as the Chairman of the Technology, Information, Forecasting and Assessment Council (TIFAC).

Dr. Kalam played a significant role in India's Pokharan-II nuclear test that was conducted in 1998.

In November 1999, Dr. Kalam was appointed as the Chief Scientific Advisor to the Govt. of India.
Later, in November 2001 he Joined Anna University at Chennai as a Professor of Technology and Societal Transformation.

Dr. Kalam—A Great Leader

When Dr. Kalam was working at the Rocket launching station in Thumba, there were around 70 scientists working under his leadership. To get success in their work and plan the scientists used to work for 12 to 18 hours daily. They could hardly spare any time for their families.

One day, a scientist came to Dr. Kalam and said, "Sir, I've promised my kids to take them to the exhibition going on in the town. So, I want to leave at 5.30 pm today, if you permit."

Dr. Kalam accepted his request and permitted him to leave at 5.30 pm. The scientist got engaged in his work. But when he finished the work it was almost 8.00 pm. He felt very bad that he had broken the promise given to his kids. Dr. Kalam was not in the office at that time.

In a Sad and tired mood, when he reached home he saw that his children were not at home. He asked to his wife about them. She replied, "Your Boss came here around 5.00 pm and took our kids for the exhibition."

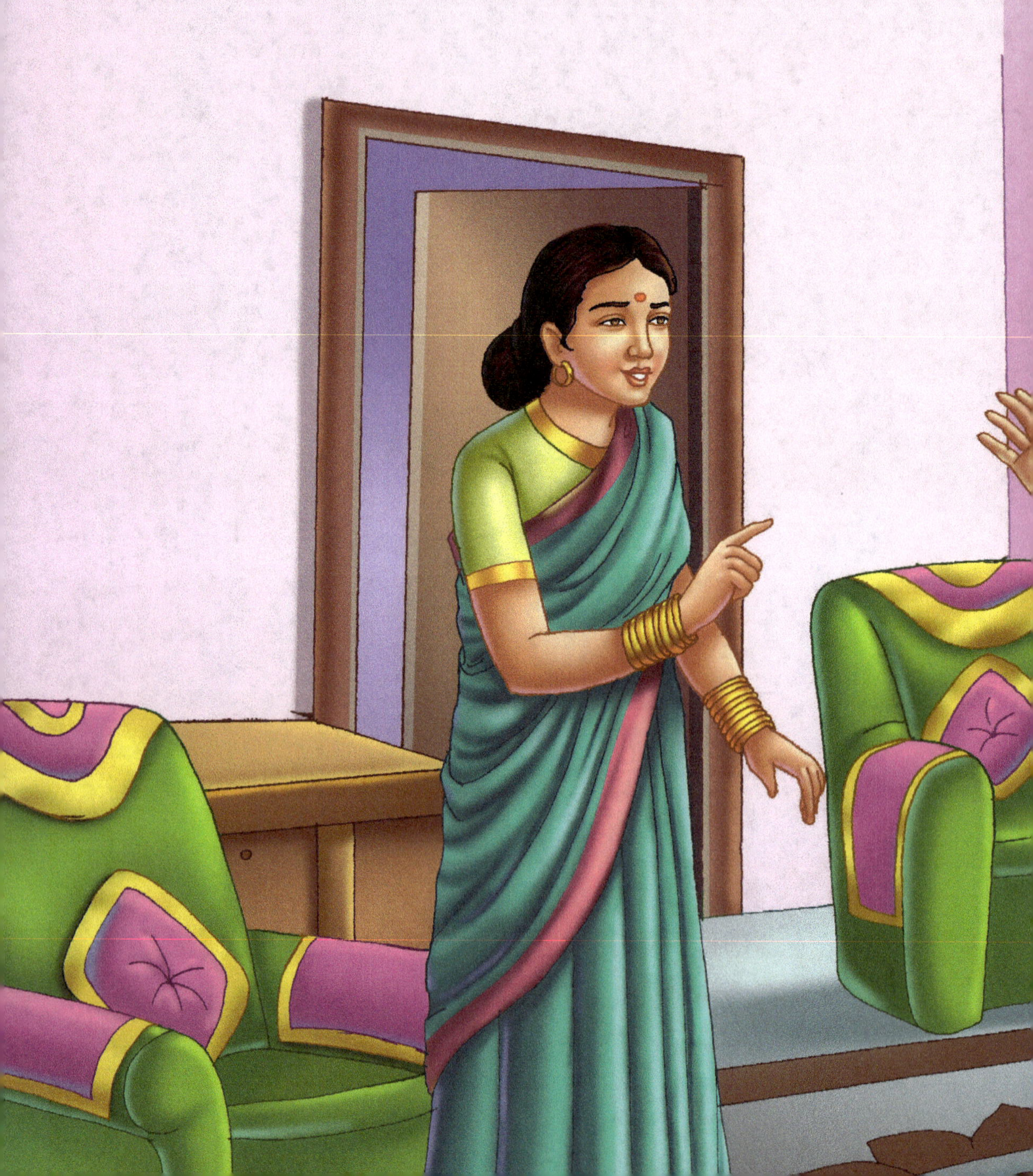

The scientist was overwhelmed by the sweet gesture of his boss. Actually, Dr. Kalam saw that the scientist was engrossed in a very important work. And, he didn't want to disappoint the kids. So, he decided to take his children on his behalf for the exhibition.

Such an understanding and caring boss was Dr. Kalam.

Dr. Kalam as the President of India

The entire nation was surprised when the ruling NDA Government nominated Dr. Kalam—the famous scientist—as their candidate for the President elections. He won the election by huge margin and became the 11th President of India on 25th July 2002.

In his speech during the oath taking ceremony, Dr. Kalam said that we should be proud of our country, "In the last 50 years, India has made many achievements in the fields of food production, health sector, higher education, media & mass communication, information technology, science and defence. In spite of these advancements, a large population is still struggling with the problems like poverty, unemployment, diseases and lack of education."

Dr. Kalam expressed his vision to eradicate all the problems from the country and making it the strongest nation one day.

During his tenure, Dr. Kalam worked especially in the fields of science and education. He was remained as an approachable and humble President. He is very fond of the children and is always concerned for their development and welfare. He aimed to make India a scientifically strong nation and always tries to ignite the spark in the minds of Indian citizens.

Dr. Kalam has a multifaceted personality. Apart from being a great scientist, he is also interested in the field of arts and culture. He has written many books including his autobiography, 'Wings of Fire'. Some of his famous books are: 'Scientist to President', 'Ignited Minds: Unleashing the Power Within India', 'India 2020' etc.

He has also written Tamil poetry. Dr. Kalam is good at playing the Indian musical instrument 'Veena'.

Dr. Kalam has three visions. His first vision is freedom. He said that our country was ruled by many and remained dependent for a long period but we the Indians respect other's freedom, thus India has great values and culture.

Dr. Kalam's second vision is development. He said that though we have achieved a lot in the last few years, but we need to have more development, especially in the fields of education, science and technology.

His third vision is that India must be strong and emerge as a super power. It should stand up to the world and show its strength.

Dr. Kalam wants to make India an advanced and technologically developed nation. In his book, 'India 2020', he has mentioned an action plan to make India a knowledge superpower and a developed nation by the year 2020.

Dr. Kalam has been awarded with Bharat Ratna (1997), Padma Vibhushan (1990), Padma Bhushan (1981) and also received many more prestigious honours and awards.

He is presently the Chancellor of the Indian Institute of Space and Technology and also works as a professor at Anna University (Chennai) and as a visiting faculty in many academic and research institutes through out the country.

In May 2011, Dr. Kalam started a new mission for the Indian youth. 'What Can I Give Movement', is a unique mission to inculcate the Universal spirit of giving in the youth.

For years, Dr. Kalam has been inspiring many lives, especially the youth and children. He is the ocean of knowledge. We should draw inspiration from his life and must work to make India- a strongest nation.

On July 27, 2015, Dr. Kalam died after collapsing, while delivering a lecture at IIM, Shillong, Meghalaya. He was 83. The whole Nation mourned on his death, and paid homage, includes the President, the PM and other dignitaries, to him.

Dr Sarvapalli Radhakrishnan
The Great Indian Philosopher

Dr Sarvapalli Radhakrishnan is known to be a great thinker, philosopher, educationist, scholar and statesman of India. His birthday, 5th September, is celebrated in India as Teachers' Day every year. He was the first Vice President of India from the year 1952 to 1962. And in 1962, he was elected as the second President of India.

Birth and Early Years of
Dr S. Radhakrishnan's Life

Dr S. Radhakrishnan was born on 5th September 1888 in a town named Tiruttani in Tamilnadu, 84 Kms. to the North West Madras (now Chennai) in a poor Telugu Brahmin family. His parents were Sarvapalli Veeraswami and Sitamma.

His father was a subordinate revenue official in the service of a local Zamindar (landlord).

Dr S. Radhakrishnan got his primary education at a high school in Tiruttani. His parents recognised his talents and tried their best to give him good education. In 1896, he was moved to the Hermansburg Evangelical Lutheral Mission School in Tirupati.

Dr S. Radhakrishnan was a brilliant student. He received many scholarships and awards in his student life. He joined Voorheese College in Vellore. Then, he joined Madras Christian College. In 1906, he got his postgraduate degree in Philosophy from there.

Dr S. Radhakrishnan's family had many financial constraints. He studied Philosophy by chance and not by choice. He got the books of Philosophy from one of his elder cousins who passed out from the same college. So, he decided to study the subject. But later on, he got very much interested in the subject and wrote many acclaimed works in Philosophy.

When Dr S. Radhakrishnan was 16-years old, he got married to his distant cousin named Sivakamu. The couple had five daughters and a son.

Professional Life of Dr S. Radhakrishnan

In 1909, he was appointed at the Department of Philosophy in Madras Presidency College. Thereafter in 1918, he was appointed as a professor of Philosophy in the University of Mysore.

Dr S. Radhakrishnan wrote many articles in Philosophy journals. He was highly influenced by the teachings of Rabindra Nath Tagore. His first book was 'The Philosophy of Rabindra Nath Tagore'. The second book that he wrote was 'The Reign of Religion in Contemporary Philosophy'.

In the year 1921, Dr S. Radhakrishnan got the chair of King George V, as the Professor of Philosophy at the Department of Mental and Moral Science in the University of Calcutta. He represented the University of Calcutta at the Congress of Universities in the British Empire 1926. He also represented the University at the International Congress of Philosophy at Harvard University in the same year.

In 1929, Dr S. Radhakrishnan was invited to deliver a lecture at Harris Manchester College, Oxford. His lecture was soon published in the form of a book, 'An Idealist View of Life'.

And soon, he was invited to take post of Principal at Harris Manchester College. During this period, he got an opportunity to deliver many important lectures. He created a bridge between East and West and explained the philosophical systems of all the traditions to people.

Dr S. Radhakrishnan acted as the Vice Chancellor of Andhra University from 1931 to 1936. In the year 1936, he was elected as a fellow of All Souls College. He was named as the 'Spalding Professor of Eastern Religions and Ethics' at Oxford University.

In 1939, Pt. Madan Mohan Malviya invited Dr S. Radhakrishnan to succeed him as a Vice Chancellor of the Banaras Hindu University (BHU). He worked at BHU till January 1948.

After India's independence in 1947, Dr S. Radhakrishnan represented the country at UNESCO. Later, he also acted as the Ambassador of India to Soviet Union. He was also elected to the Constituent Assembly of India.

In 1952, Dr S. Radhakrishnan was elected as the first Vice President of India. He became the President of India in the year 1962. He occupied the honourable position till 1967.

When Dr S. Radhakrishnan became the President of India, the entire world was pleased. He was one of the greatest philosophers of the world, Bertrand Russell said,

"It is an honour to Philosophy that Dr S. Radhakrishnan is the President of India and I, as a philosopher, take special pleasure in this. Pleto aspired for philosophers to become kings and it is a tribute to India to have a philosopher as a President.

Even working on the post of the President, Dr S. Radhakrishnan was extremely humble. During his work tenure, people from all the sections of society were welcome at Rashtrapati Bhavan. He listened to each and every person and addressed all the issues. He tried his best to resolve the issues of the society.

Dr S. Radhakrishnan wrote many significant books on Indian traditions and culture. He popularised the greatness of Indian traditions, teachings and Hinduism in western countries.

Dr S. Radhakrishnan earned many prestigious honours and titles for his extraordinary services in the field of education. He was honoured by the knighthood in 1931. He was also honoured by the Bharat Ratna in 1954, and the Order of Merit in 1963.

In 1961, Dr S. Radhakrishnan received the Peace Prize of the German Book Trade. He also received the Templeton Prize in 1975. He donated the entire amount of the Templeton Prize to the Oxford University. In 1989, the University started giving 'Dr S. Radhakrishnan scholarships' in his memory.

Many authors and educationists all around the world were influenced by Dr S. Radhakrishnan and his philosophies. There are also some books written on his life and his ideas.

Dr S. Radhakrishnan's Birthday is celebrated as Teachers' Day

Dr S. Radhakrishnan said, "The teachers should be the best minds of the country." In his opinion, teachers should not only instruct the students but also earn their affection. He also believed that respect for teachers should be earned, not demanded.

Dr S. Radhakrishnan not only imparted knowledge to his students but also earned their true love and respect for his unique style of teachings. He was very popular among the students.

TEACHER'S DAY

When Dr S. Radhakrishnan was leaving the University of Mysore, his students organised a grand farewell for him. He was taken to the railway station in a flower-decked carriage pulled by his students.

There is an interesting incident about how the celebration of Teachers' Day started on Dr S. Radhakrishnan's birthday. When he was elected as the President of India, some of his students asked for his permission to celebrate his birthday.

Dr S. Radhakrishnan believed that teachers play a very important role in shaping the future of the students and the country.

Dr S. Radhakrishnan said to his students, "Instead of celebrating my birthday separately, it would be my proud privilege if September 5 will be observed as Teachers' Day." He asked his students to dedicate "Teachers' Day" not only to him but also to all the teachers.

Since then every year, Dr S. Radhakrishnan's birthday, 5th September, is celebrated as Teachers' Day all across the country. All the schools, colleges and institutions celebrate the day in the honour of the great man and all the teachers.

Dr S. Radhakrishnan regarded the teaching as the noblest profession. He believed that the progress of any nation depends largely on the teachers. Teachers dedicate their lives to educate their students.

He once said, "The aim of education is not the acquisition of information, although important, or acquisition of technical skills, though essential in modern society but the development of that bent of mind, that attitude of reason, that spirit of democracy which will make us responsible citizens."

Last Years of Dr S. Radhakrishnan's Life

Dr S. Radhakrishnan retired from the public life in 1967. He spent the last years of his life in his house in Madras (Chennai). He breathed his last at the age of 87 on 17th April 1975.

His death was a big loss for the country. His absence created a vacuum in the field of education and philosophy. He is still remembered for his valuable work all over the world. His birthday is celebrated with great enthusiasm as Teachers' Day all across India.

Dr S. Radhakrishnan dedicated his whole life in educating and empowering people. His only motto was to make India a wonderful nation standing on a strong foundation of education. He believed that only education could change and shape the future of the entire nation.

We can learn a lot from the great life of Dr S. Radhakrishnan. We should always remember his significance and efforts in keeping the foundation of the Indian education system.